First World War
and Army of Occupation
War Diary
France, Belgium and Germany

14 DIVISION
43 Infantry Brigade,
Brigade Machine Gun Company
16 February 1916 - 28 February 1918

WO95/1910/5

The Naval & Military Press Ltd
www.nmarchive.com
Published in association with The National Archives

Published by

The Naval & Military Press Ltd

Unit 10 Ridgewood Industrial Park,

Uckfield, East Sussex,

TN22 5QE England

Tel: +44 (0) 1825 749494

www.naval-military-press.com

www.nmarchive.com

This diary has been reprinted in facsimile from the original. Any imperfections are inevitably reproduced and the quality may fall short of modern type and cartographic standards.

© **Crown Copyright**
Images reproduced by permission of The National Archives, London, England, 2015.

Contents

Document type	Place/Title	Date From	Date To
Heading	WO95/1910/5 14 Div-43 Inf Bde Bde MG Coy Feb 1916-Feb 1918.		
Heading	14th Division 43rd Infy Bde 43rd Machine Gun Coy. Feb 1916-Feb 1918		
Miscellaneous	DAG 3rd Echelon	01/04/1916	01/04/1916
War Diary	Houtkerque	16/02/1916	22/02/1916
War Diary	Vignacourt	23/02/1916	23/02/1916
War Diary	Beauval	24/02/1916	24/02/1916
War Diary	Humbercourt	25/02/1916	28/02/1916
War Diary	Bernville	29/02/1916	04/03/1916
War Diary	Dainville	05/03/1916	30/04/1916
Miscellaneous	DAG 3rd Echelon GHQ	01/06/1916	01/06/1916
War Diary	Dainville	01/05/1916	31/05/1916
Miscellaneous	D.A.G. 3rd Echelon G.H.Q.	01/07/1916	01/07/1916
War Diary	Dainville	01/06/1916	18/06/1916
War Diary	Arras	19/06/1916	30/06/1916
Heading	War Diary. For July 1916. 43rd Brigade Machine Gun Company. Vol 5.		
Miscellaneous	A.G. Office Machine Gun Corps Section Base.	31/07/1916	31/07/1916
War Diary	Arras Ref Maps 1/10000	01/07/1916	02/07/1916
War Diary	Arras 51 B N.W. 3	03/07/1916	23/07/1916
War Diary	Arras	24/07/1916	29/07/1916
War Diary	Warluzel	30/07/1916	30/07/1916
War Diary	Remaisnil	31/07/1916	31/07/1916
Heading	43rd Brigade. 14th Division. 43rd Brigade Machine Gun Company August 1916.		
Heading	War Diary For 43rd Machine Gun Company August 1916. (Volume)		
War Diary	Remaisnil Ref Map. France Lens II 1:100,000.	01/08/1916	07/08/1916
War Diary	Albert	08/08/1917	17/08/1917
War Diary	Ref Map No X 13 XV Corps	18/08/1916	19/08/1916
War Diary	Camp F14 B Central Sheet 1:20,000 Montauban	20/08/1916	21/08/1916
War Diary	Camp Near Fricourt	21/08/1916	25/08/1916
War Diary	Montauban	26/08/1916	31/08/1916
Miscellaneous	A.G.s Office Machine Gun Corps Section Base.	03/09/1916	03/09/1916
Miscellaneous	DAG. 3rd Echelon	01/10/1916	01/10/1916
War Diary	Hornoy 1/100,000 Sheet 16.	01/09/1916	11/09/1916
War Diary	Map Albert 1:40,000	12/09/1916	17/09/1916
War Diary	Ribemont	18/09/1916	18/09/1916
War Diary	Ref Map Albert	19/09/1916	21/09/1916
War Diary	Sus-St-Leger Ref Map Lens	22/09/1916	25/09/1916
War Diary	Arras. H Sector	26/09/1916	30/09/1916
Heading	War Diary of 43rd Machine Gun Company. October 1st-October 31st.		
War Diary	Arras	01/10/1916	26/10/1916
War Diary	Lattre St Quentin	27/10/1916	27/10/1916
War Diary	Beaufort	28/10/1916	31/10/1916
Map	British Front From High Wood To Ginchy		
Miscellaneous	15a		

Heading	War Diary of 43rd M.G. Coy From 1st November 1916 To 30th November 1916 (Volume 9)		
War Diary	Beaufort	01/11/1916	30/11/1916
Heading	War Diary 43rd Machine Gun Company December 1916 Volume 10		
War Diary	Houvin-Houvigneul	01/12/1916	14/12/1916
War Diary	Grand Rullecourt	15/12/1916	15/12/1916
War Diary	Wanquetin	16/12/1916	16/12/1916
War Diary	Arras	17/12/1916	31/12/1916
Heading	43rd Machine Gun Company War Diary January 1917 Volume 11		
War Diary	Arras	01/01/1917	31/01/1917
Heading	War Diary 43rd Machine Gun Company Volume 12 February 1917.		
War Diary	Arras	01/02/1917	28/02/1917
Heading	War Diary. 43rd Machine Gun Company. For Month Of March 1917. Volume. 13.		
War Diary	Arras	01/03/1917	20/03/1917
War Diary	East Of Arras	21/03/1917	24/03/1917
War Diary	Arras	25/03/1917	26/03/1917
War Diary	Dainville	27/03/1917	31/03/1917
War Diary	War Diary 43rd Machine Gun Company Volume 14 April 1917. Vol 14		
War Diary	Dainville	01/04/1917	09/04/1917
War Diary	E. Of Arras	09/04/1917	11/04/1917
War Diary	Arras	11/04/1917	14/04/1917
War Diary	Sus St Leger	15/04/1917	23/04/1917
War Diary	Basseux	24/04/1917	26/04/1917
War Diary	Ronville	27/04/1917	30/04/1917
Heading	War Diary. For Month Of May 1917. 43rd Machine Gun Company. Volume. 15.		
War Diary	Ronville	01/05/1917	02/05/1917
War Diary	Wancourt	03/05/1917	04/05/1917
War Diary	In the Line	05/05/1917	09/05/1917
War Diary	East Of Wancourt	05/05/1917	09/05/1917
War Diary	East Of Wancourt	05/05/1917	14/05/1917
War Diary	East Of Wancourt	10/05/1917	14/05/1917
War Diary	Beaurains	15/05/1917	25/05/1917
War Diary	N. of Neuville Vitasse	25/05/1917	31/05/1917
Heading	War Diary 43rd Machine Gun Company June 1917 Volume 16		
War Diary	N. of Neuville Vitasse	01/06/1917	02/06/1917
War Diary	E. Of Wancourt	03/06/1917	11/06/1917
War Diary	Beaurains	12/06/1917	12/06/1917
War Diary	Beaumetz	13/06/1917	13/06/1917
War Diary	Gaudiempre	14/06/1917	14/06/1917
War Diary	Authie	15/06/1917	30/06/1917
Heading	War Diary of 43rd Machine Gun Company From July 1st 1917 To July 31st 1917 (Vol. 17)		
Miscellaneous	To/H.Q. 43 Inf Bde	01/08/1917	01/08/1917
War Diary	Authie	01/07/1917	09/07/1917
War Diary	Gezaincourt	10/07/1917	11/07/1917
War Diary	Bailleul	11/07/1917	12/07/1917
War Diary	Croix De Poperinghe	13/07/1917	31/07/1917
Heading	War Diary 43rd Machine Gun Company August 1917 Volume 18		

War Diary	Croix De Poperinghe	01/08/1917	05/08/1917
War Diary	Caestre	06/08/1917	14/08/1917
War Diary	N.W. Abeele	15/08/1917	16/08/1917
War Diary	N. Dickebusch	17/08/1917	20/08/1917
War Diary	E Of Hooge	21/08/1917	23/08/1917
War Diary	E Of Hooge	22/08/1917	24/08/1917
War Diary	Ouderdom	25/08/1917	31/08/1917
Heading	War Diary. 43rd Machine Gun Company. September 1917. Volume. 19.		
War Diary	Roukloshille Area	01/09/1917	04/09/1917
War Diary	E Of Steenwerck	05/09/1917	14/09/1917
War Diary	Neuve Eglise	15/09/1917	20/09/1917
War Diary	E Of Messines	20/09/1917	28/09/1917
War Diary	Ravelsberg Area	29/09/1917	30/09/1917
Heading	War Diary. October 1917. 43rd Machine Gun Company. Volume 20		
War Diary	Ravelsberg Area	01/10/1917	05/10/1917
War Diary	N. of Westoutre	06/10/1917	08/10/1917
War Diary	N.W. Of Laclytte	09/10/1917	13/10/1917
War Diary	W Of Polderhoek Chateau	14/10/1917	24/10/1917
War Diary	Berthen Area	25/10/1917	31/10/1917
Heading	War Diary. 43rd Machine Gun Company. November 1917. Volume 21.		
War Diary	Berthen Area	01/11/1917	13/11/1917
War Diary	Westbecourt	14/11/1917	30/11/1917
Heading	War Diary. 43rd Machine Gun Company. December 1917. Volume 22.		
War Diary	Westbecourt	01/12/1917	03/12/1917
War Diary	St. Jean	04/12/1917	08/12/1917
War Diary	N.E. Passchendale	09/12/1917	16/12/1917
War Diary	Brandhoek	17/12/1917	21/12/1917
War Diary	N.E. Passchendale	22/12/1917	28/12/1917
War Diary	Westbecourt	29/12/1917	31/12/1917
Heading	War Diary of 43rd Machine Gun Coy For January 1918. Volume 33.		
War Diary	Westbecourt	01/01/1918	01/01/1918
War Diary	Tatinghem	02/01/1918	02/01/1918
War Diary	Brays/Somme	03/01/1918	22/01/1918
War Diary	Gillaucourt	23/01/1918	23/01/1918
War Diary	Guiscard	24/01/1918	24/01/1918
War Diary	Flavy-Le-Martel	25/01/1918	25/01/1918
War Diary	Remigny	26/01/1918	31/01/1918
Heading	War Diary. 43rd Machine Gun Coy February 1918. Volume 24.		
War Diary	Moy Sector	01/02/1918	25/02/1918
War Diary	Jussy	26/02/1918	28/02/1918

WO95/1910-5

14 Div - 43 Inf Bde

Bde M G Coy

Feb 1916 - Feb 1918

14TH DIVISION
43RD INFY BDE

43RD MACHINE GUN COY.
FEB 1916-FEB 1918

Ref M.9.L.3

To/ DAG
3rd Echelon

Herewith War Diary (original)
of this Company from date of
formation to 31/3/16.

J de Hughton Capt. o.n.g
1/4/16   43rd Bde M.G. Coy.

Feb 16

Feb 18

WAR DIARY or INTELLIGENCE SUMMARY

Army Form C. 2118.

43 Bde M. G. Coy.

(Erase heading not required.)

Place	Date Feb 16	Hour	Summary of Events and Information	Remarks and references to Appendices
HOUTKERQUE	16.	—	43 Bde M.G. Coy assembled and was billeted at HOUTKERQUE.	
	17.	—	Nil	
	18.	—	Company was inspected by B.G. Commdg, 43. L. I. Bde.	
	19.	—	Route march	
	20.	—	Gun drill etc.	
	21.	—	ditto	
	22.	—	Marched to ESQUERBECQUES and entrained at 12.10 pm for AMIENS.	
VIGNACOURT	23	—	detrained 23rd Feb about 3 a.m. and proceeded by bus to VIGNACOURT. VIGNACOURT. Men billeted in their billets	
BEAUVAL	24	—	about 4.30 a.m. received orders to move by march route to BEAUVAL on the way back to the trenches once more. Our much needed rest finished after one day. Snow lay all day & had a hard march, arrived in billets 5pm	
HUMBERCOURT	25	—	marched at 11 a.m. for HUMBERCOURT via DOULLENS roads very bad for transport on account of ice etc. arrived, marched in to billets at 4pm. transport 11.30 p.m.	
"	26.	—	Rest.	
"	27	—	ditto	

Army Form C. 2118.

WAR DIARY
or
INTELLIGENCE SUMMARY
(Erase heading not required.)

Instructions regarding War Diaries and Intelligence Summaries are contained in F.S. Regs., Part II. and the Staff Manual respectively. Title Pages will be prepared in manuscript.

Place	Date	Hour	Summary of Events and Information	Remarks and references to Appendices
"	28.		Marched at 9 a.m. to BERNVILLE. Via GOUY-EN-ARTOIS. Transport by ARRAS Rd. arrived 1 p.m. into billets by 3 pm. delay due to lack of billets.	
BERNVILLE	29		Clean up generally. O.C. Company and his Officers went over to DAINVILLE to reconnoitre the new line at ACHICOURT and AGNY, made arrangements to take over 10 gun emplacements from 65th Inf. Bde (French)	
"	March 1st		Ten guns and 4 officers (Lts HAYES, WOOD, ANDREWS and BOTTOM) went up into the line. Company H.Q. at BERNVILLE. Advanced HQ at AGNY.	
"	2.		Nothing to report.	
"	3.		Nothing to report.	
"	4.		Received orders to move personnel of company into billets on the main ARRAS – AMIENS road near DAINVILLE. (L 35 B 4.5. Sheet 51C FRANCE) Transport to remain in BERNVILLE.	
DAINVILLE	5		Nothing to report.	
"	6		42 Bde M.G. Coy. took over 3 gun positions, our 9 43 BM.G.Coy remained in the line in 6 different positions, leaving 8 guns in and 8 out.	not
"	7.		Dispositions unchanged. Nothing to report. Personnel relieved in hereafter.	
"	8.		Nothing to report.	

WAR DIARY
or
INTELLIGENCE SUMMARY
(Erase heading not required.)

Army Form C. 2118.

Place	Date	Hour	Summary of Events and Information	Remarks and references to Appendices
"	9		Nothing to report	
	10			
	11			
	12		LT HAYES accidentally killed by accidence of gun emplacement.	
	13		Nothing to report. Personnel relieved from trenches night of 14/15th.	
	14			
	15		Nothing to report.	
	16		New emplacement completed in hand A+(GB) / 4th E of railway and gun put in.	
	17		Nothing to report.	
	18		Work commenced on new emplacement in Railway line immediately South of A Group	
	19		Work continued on above. Nothing to report.	
	20		Nothing to report.	
	21		M. Gun. personnel in trenches relieved.	

Army Form C. 2118.

WAR DIARY
or
INTELLIGENCE SUMMARY
(Erase heading not required.)

Instructions regarding War Diaries and Intelligence Summaries are contained in F. S. Regs., Part II. and the Staff Manual respectively. Title Pages will be prepared in manuscript.

Place	Date	Hour	Summary of Events and Information	Remarks and references to Appendices
	22		New emplacement on railway line, covering the hostility and also S side of AGNY completed. Gun put in.	
	23		Nothing to report.	
	24		" " "	
	25		" " "	
	26		" " "	
	27		New emplacement in B3a completed sufficiently to be manned. Gun taken on this position which has a good field of fire along our front line to the East. Personnel remaining gun released.	
	28		Post in in AGNY defence (A2) originally started by the French completed stocked and manned.	
	29		Dug out for officers & men in AGNY finished and made proof against H.E. up to 5.9.	
	30		Nothing to report.	
	31			

2449 Wt. W14957/Mg0 750,000 1/16 J.B.C. & A. Forms/C.2118/12.

Army Form C. 2118.

WAR DIARY
or
INTELLIGENCE SUMMARY

(Erase heading not required.)

43 Bde M.G. Coy. Vol 2

Instructions regarding War Diaries and Intelligence Summaries are contained in F. S. Regs., Part II. and the Staff Manual respectively. Title Pages will be prepared in manuscript.

Place	Date	Hour	Summary of Events and Information	Remarks and references to Appendices
DAINVILLE	April 1		Gun positions in the line generally shelled throughout	
	2.			
	3.		Nothing to report.	
	4.		Teams relieved	
	5.		Nothing to report	
	6.		" " "	
	7.		" " "	
	8.		" " "	
	9.		" " "	
	10.		8th M.G. Battery took over his gun positions to relieve pressure on our teams	
	11.		Teams relieved.	
	12.		New position near junction of Q.B.3 & Q.B.1 commenced	
	13.		Gun position carried on with.	
	14.		" " " "	
	15.		New position finished and occupied by 9th M.M.G. who handed back our other position to us.	
	16.		Heavy Artillery bombarded enemy front line. His own M. guns fired throughout the night on portions of line bombarded during the day.	

Army Form C. 2118.

WAR DIARY
or
INTELLIGENCE SUMMARY
(Erase heading not required.)

Instructions regarding War Diaries and Intelligence Summaries are contained in F. S. Regs., Part II. and the Staff Manual respectively. Title Pages will be prepared in manuscript.

Place	Date	Hour	Summary of Events and Information	Remarks and references to Appendices
"	17	—	Nothing to report.	
	18	—	Tram Relieved.	
	19	—		
	20			
	21			
	22		No (King?) to report, some trent work, night firing by 3 guns laid indirect.	
	23			
	24			
	25		Trams relieved	
	26		Nothing to report.	
: :	27		Cuckoo heard at 9.15 am. nr ACTICOURT!	
	28		Nothing of interest to report, 3 guns fire each night on roads and	
	29		selected points such as dumps etc. The firing seems to have	
	30		suppressed enemy machine gun fire by night.	

J. M. M. Phles Capt
43 Battery ? . Cn.

30/4/16.

2449 Wt. W14957/M90 750,000 1/16 J.B.C. & A. Forms/C.2118/12.

D.A.G.
3rd Echelon
G.H.Q.

Herewith War Diary (original) Vol III
of this company from 1/5/16 to 31/5/16

[signature] Capt
Cmdg 43rd B.M.G. Coy.

43RD BRIGADE
MACHINE. GUN
COMPANY.
No. MGL. 64
Date 1/6/16

Army Form C. 2118.

Vol. 3

WAR DIARY
or
INTELLIGENCE SUMMARY

(Erase heading not required.) 43 Bde M. Gun. Company.

Vol 3

XIV

Place	Date	Hour	Summary of Events and Information	Remarks and references to Appendices
DAINVILLE	MAY 1.	—	Nothing to report	
	2.	—	Teams relieved in the trenches	
	3.	—	Nothing to report.	
	4.	—	One gun laid by day for aircraft claims to have struck and driven off Enemy aeroplane. The machine was seen to descend hurriedly in the Enemy's lines after emitting large amount of smoke. It at any rate retired hastily. No other anti-aircraft guns had fired.	
	5.		Nothing to report.	
	6.		At 12.55 am the order "Stand to" was given to the 4 guns in the A.G.N.Y defences as a practice Stand To. The guns were carried to their emplacements as ammunition (except 8 belts always kept in each emplacement) Shown paid site. The fur most gun was ready to fire in 12 minutes.	
	7.) 8.)		Nothing to report.	
	9.		Relief	
	10		Moderately heavy shelling, no casualties to the Company. Much improving trenches. mol. by night.	

WAR DIARY
or
INTELLIGENCE SUMMARY
(Erase heading not required.)

Army Form C. 2118.

Place	Date	Hour	Summary of Events and Information	Remarks and references to Appendices
"	11		Nothing to report.	
	12.		Another practice "Stand to". Agny defences very satisfactory.	
	13.		Quiet day — One man accidentally killed by explosion of old "flare" shell which he was apparently trying to open, — with fatal results.	
	14.		Nothing to report.	
	15.		Gun emplacement no 9 was shelled about 5.30pm, but no casualties or damage to any extent. It was not considered that the shelling was deliberately at this emplacement, but at the truck adjoining in which men had been working during the day. Team returned later.	
	16.		O.C. Anti-aircraft selected new site as an alternative position to N09.	
	17.		New emplacement commenced.	
	18.		2/Lt. SYERS joined the Company from England.	
	19.		"Gas Alert". Nothing to report.	
	20.		Nothing to report.	
	21.		Work on new emplacement.	
	22.			

Army Form C. 2118.

WAR DIARY
or
INTELLIGENCE SUMMARY
(Erase heading not required.)

Instructions regarding War Diaries and Intelligence Summaries are contained in F. S. Regs., Part II. and the Staff Manual respectively. Title Pages will be prepared in manuscript.

Place	Date	Hour	Summary of Events and Information	Remarks and references to Appendices
	23.		Relief: Sake men sent up to his gun in around of enemy mine has not been located. Was 2 gun crews the unspotted area.	
	24.			
	25.		Nothing to report, but continuous new Vg emplacement.	
	26.			
	27.		— — — —	
	28.		New emplacement in AGNY VILLAGE commenced.	
	29.		Nothing to report.	
	30.			
	31.		About 1.15 a.m. enemy opened heavy bombardment. V15 emplacement on the Railway line was struck by a kind shell. The in pistol support was Cal. and we have nowhere to see damage to any of the guns in the line.	

[signature]
43 Bn M. Gun Coy

To
D.A.G.
3rd Echelon
G.H.Q.

Herewith War Diary (original) Vol 4 of this Company from 1-6-16 to 30-6-16

[signature] Capt
cmdg 43rd B.M.G.Coy.

43rd BRIGADE
MACHINE GUN
COMPANY
MGL 104
1-7-16

Army Form C. 2118.

June
Vol. 4
Vol 4

XIV

WAR DIARY
or
INTELLIGENCE SUMMARY

(Erase heading not required.)

4 3 Bde. M. Gun. Coy.

Place	Date June	Hour	Summary of Events and Information	Remarks and references to Appendices
DAINVILLE	1. to 12th		Much night firing - both carried on with day wk for new M.g. position. also new concrete position in AGNY defences, otherwise nothing to report of any importance.	
	13th 14th 15th		Nothing to report.	
	16th		Billets and Brigade H.Q. shelled with 4.2 h.e., one shell through my G. billet at 6.15 a.m. - Decision to get new billet in ARRAS - DOULLENS road becoming unhealthy -	
	17th		Arrive new billet by Tom bugn and shewed moving in when order received that we were to be relieved on 18th by 164th Bn. M.G. Coy and were then to proceed to billet in ARRAS	
	18th		Relief took place accordingly - Division now to relieve 15th & 95th Bde. M.G. Coys on 21st. 11 Guns to go in sector held by 15th and 5 in that held by 95th.	

Army Form C. 2118.

WAR DIARY
or
INTELLIGENCE SUMMARY
(Erase heading not required.)

Instructions regarding War Diaries and Intelligence Summaries are contained in F. S. Regs., Part II. and the Staff Manual respectively. Title Pages will be prepared in manuscript.

Place	Date JUNE	Hour	Summary of Events and Information	Remarks and references to Appendices
ARRAS	19th 20th		New line reconnoitred and gun positions decided on. 5 guns in I Sector and 11 in J1 & J2.	
	21st		Relieved 16th Bde R.E. Coy during the afternoon and the 95th Bde R.E. Coy at night.	
	22		Nothing to report.	
	23		Reconnoitred right sector (I) with view to selecting new positions for 3 guns from left sector, with the object of covering J1 & J2 from South of R. SCARPE in I sector.	
	24 25		In accordance with above, reconnoitred and decided where this 3 guns to be taken from to left sectors.	
	26		Laid 3 guns with direct-aim to fire in enemy wire which is being cut by day by R.F.A. by night	
	27		Fused in three S.I.G. in I.Sub Section for use emplacements and arranged working parties in conjunction with O/C. 61 F. Coy. R.E.	

Army Form C. 2118.

WAR DIARY
or
INTELLIGENCE SUMMARY

(Erase heading not required.)

Instructions regarding War Diaries and Intelligence Summaries are contained in F. S. Regs., Part II. and the Staff Manual respectively. Title Pages will be prepared in manuscript.

Place	Date	Hour	Summary of Events and Information	Remarks and references to Appendices
ARRAS	28 29		Nothing to report. Aeroplane firing by 3 guns on foks in enemy wire continues.	
	30		New emplacements in the Thin continued	

J. W. Hopkins Calder
Comdg 143rd Bde M.G. Coy
30/6/16

WAR DIARY.

for

JULY 1916.

43rd Brigade Machine Gun Company.

10

M.G. Officer
Machine Gun Corps Section
Base.

Herewith original War Diary of the company under my command, Vol. 5 from 1/7/16 to 31/7/16.

J McHoughton
Capt.
Comdg 43rd M.G.Coy.

4580 BRIGADE
MACHINE GUN
COMPANY.
No. MG&R2
Date 31-7-16.

Army Form C. 2118.

WAR DIARY
or
INTELLIGENCE SUMMARY

(Erase heading not required.) A 3 Bde. M. Gun. Coy. Volume 5

Place	Date July	Hour	Summary of Events and Information	Remarks and references to Appendices
ARRAS	1		Arras was shelled in the early morning. Our artillery was bombarding Villes. No M.Guns firing tonight because of patrols going out. Nothing to report.	
Ref Maps 1/10,000	2		Intense bombardment. Nothing to report.	
ARRAS 51 B'n M.3	3		One gun in front line trench J92 knocked out by hostile shell fire. One man wounded and entrenchment demolished. Taken to open position in L.P. 91 temporarily.	
	4		Nothing to report. Night firing when our our whistle to be very successful. Guards (?) heard.	
	5			
	6		Nothing to report. Used night firing. New emplacements progressing.	
	7 to 21		Nothing to report. On morning of 21 July received orders to hand over to 42 Bde M.G. Coy. gun positions in I sub-sector. The 5th Bgn. K.S.L.I. to relieve 6th Som. L.I. in this sector. Took over O.C. 42 Bde M.Gun. Coy. round these positions. The two new emplacements are dug outs nearly finished.	
	22 "			
	23.		5 guns in I sector relieved by 42 Bde M.G. Coy. 2 guns D8/M.M.G./35 relieved by 43 " " " Coy in J2 sector. Town of Arras shelled during the afternoon by 5.9 H.E.	

WAR DIARY
or
INTELLIGENCE SUMMARY
(Erase heading not required.)

Army Form C. 2118.

Place	Date	Hour	Summary of Events and Information	Remarks and references to Appendices
ARRAS	24		About 9.30 pm on the 23rd heavy hostile shell fire opened on T1, destroying Corpl in which no. 9th Company's gun was situated, the team were practically buried. Two wounded - no men hurt. His Teams 81 to 83 hrs were employed after bombing assignation's dug out surrounding two men. Enemy attempted a raid on us but his teams 81 to 83 hrs were repulsed after bombing assignation's dug out surrounding two men. New position was selected for the Sect gun & taken up.	
	25		Nothing to report.	
	26.		Received orders to handover to 62nd B.M.G. Coy & 110th M.G. Coy. 110th Coy to take over T2 and 62nd Coy T1.	
	27.		Relief carried out by 110th Coy of guns in T2 sector, completed by 9 pm without any unusual occurrence	
	28.		Relief carried out by 62nd Coy of guns in T1 sector, completed by 11.30 am. 43rd Bn M.G. Coy proceeded to WARLUS - into billets.	
	29.		43 Inf Bde marched from AGNEZ-LES-DUISANS and WARLUS to billets

WAR DIARY
or
INTELLIGENCE SUMMARY

Army Form C. 2118.

Place	Date	Hour	Summary of Events and Information	Remarks and references to Appendices
			at WARLUZEL, SUS-ST LEGER and neighbourhood. Bde. HQ at WARLUZEL. 43 Bde M.G. Coy marched at 12 noon via WANQUETIN — FOSSEUX — BARLY — SOMBRIN to WARLUZEL. Arrived in Camp about 4.10pm after a very hot march. Men's feet suffered after being in the trenches continuously since 1st March. Received orders to march again next day.	
WARLUZEL	30.		43 Bde continued its march at 10.10am to billets at and round VILLERS L'HOPITAL. 43 Bde. HQ. Machine Gun Coy. and T.M. battery to REMAISNIL. Marched via SUS — ST. LEGER — IVERNY — LE SOUICH — BOUQMAISON — NEVILLETTE and arrived in billets at 1.30pm. Much hotter today than yesterday and 38 men fell out — all returned with exception of 1 + assisted to hospital.	
REMAISNIL	31		Day of much needed rest. Company bathed at 6.30am in R. AUTHIE. The day spent in cleaning guns — telling off sections and washing. Very hot indeed.	

J.E. McClellan
Captain
Comdg 43 Bde M. Gun. Coy.

43rd Brigade.
14th Division.

43rd BRIGADE

MACHINE GUN COMPANY.

AUGUST 1916

CONFIDENTIAL.

WAR DIARY

for

43RD MACHINE GUN COMPANY

AUGUST 1916.

(Volume   )

CONFIDENTIAL.

WAR DIARY
INTELLIGENCE SUMMARY

Army Form C. 2118.
Vol. 6.

(Erase heading not required.) 143 Bde. M.G. Coy.

Place	Date	Hour	Summary of Events and Information	Remarks and references to Appendices
RENAISNIL	August 1916 5		Coy in huts at LE MEILLARD. Spent 5 very useful days training in Combined Wire Route Marching. All men battled daily. Men classes had opportunities firing	
Ref Map	5th			
FRANCE.	6.		Coy transport left by road route to VILLERS via CANAPLES.	
LENS II. 1:100,000	7.		Coy entrained at CANDAS at 11.15am having marched from LE MEILLARD at 4.15am. Arrived MERICOURT 4pm and marched into camp about 6.30pm near ALBERT.	
ALBERT	8-9. 10-11		Ref Map 1/40,000 ALBERT E8C 9.0. Carried on company training	
	12		Took over huts 10 guns from 52.M.G.Coy in DELVILLE WOOD. Door a/c relief which was completed without casualties. (No 1 & No 3 Gun shot and killed a german. The gun itself opened fire and immediately 30-odd germans surrendered. About 90-10 dead germans were found. Nothing to report. 3 casualties (wounded) from shell fire	
	13.			
	14.		last night. No 3 gun opened fire on a german patrol on young germans pushed into the hunt and surrendered	
	15		Early in the morning relief completed without casualties. DELVILLE WOOD has been quiet in the whole of day	
	16		Nothing to report.	

Place	Date	Hour	Summary of Events and Information	Remarks and references to Appendices
	17.		Relief of 6 guns' teams completed by 8 am without incident - orders received concerning the attack to be made by 43 h.f. Bde in conjunction with other tps of 9th. III. XV + XIII Corps. Six guns of this company in two lots of 3 each under Lt MUSCHAMP + 2Lt WOOD detailed to follow the infantry & assist to consolidate the position. Each gun team consisting of 5 trained men and 3 carriers.	
R.G.M.A. N° X 13 XV Corps	18.	At 2.45 pm	At 2.45 pm 1st to 6th Bns. Som. L.I. and 6th Bn. D.C.L.I. attacked 115 enemy positions from S.18.B.3.0.8 to S.18.D.6.4. inclusive. Six guns in two sections of 3, each under an officer and the necessary other ranks were told off to assist the attacking Bns. They had orders to go up in the swept track Bn taking its objective and to take up the best position possible from which to assist in repelling any counter attacks that might be delivered. The 3 guns to co-operate with 1st Som. L.I. were under 2Lt E.V. WOOD and were given as their objective points S.18.D.7.5.-T.13.C.2.7½ - and was the junction of VAT ALLEY and BEER TRENCH. These 3 guns succeeded in reaching these points with only 1 casualty. The men lay outside DELVILLE WOOD and taking advantage of crump holes etc	

advanced in extended order at 2.30 a.m. and remained in action until relieved at 2:30 am 20 August by 42. M.G.Coy. suffering no casualties but one hope was destroyed by shell fire. Lt. E.V. WOOD was unfortunately wounded shortly after his gun had arrived in the Captured trench. Lt. E. W. MUSCHAMP took 1/6 of 1st 3 guns co-operating with the 6/DCLI and had as his objectives points S18.b.7.9 – T13.A.7.0 and the junction of HOP ALLEY with BEER TRENCH. Owing to the DCLI failing to hold on to the captured trenches the two guns had to fall back on HOP ALLEY. The team were all wounded and the gun destroyed by a Direct hit. Lt. E.W. MUSCHAMP attempted to take one gun from its position about S18.B.7.4 to the head of the Sap S18.b.9.5 unfortunately he was severely wounded in the head and all the team with the exception of one man. The remaining few under a Sergeant remained in its position about S18.b.1.7. Pte GRANT (Stretcher bearer) having volunteered to go with

WAR DIARY or INTELLIGENCE SUMMARY

Army Form C. 2118.

Place	Date	Hour	Summary of Events and Information	Remarks and references to Appendices
			three 3 guns – behaved with great gallantry & rendered first aid under continuous shelling & has been recommended for I.E. D.C.M.	
			About 10 p.m. on the 18 August 2nd Lt. J.R. BORROW was sent up with two guns to take up positions as follows S.18.c.9.5 and the junction of HOP ALLEY with BEER TRENCH, which he accomplished without any casualties in spite of severe shelling whilst on way up. During this operation Lt. ANDREWS with 4 guns had remained in the hand in DELVILLE WOOD occupied by the 6th K.O.Y.L.I., his guns kept up a steady barrage all the afternoon of the 18th and his Lewis guns about S.18.a.2.2½ caught the enemy in enfilade whilst attempting to consolidate about Hop & Ale (?) on our left in fleeting across ours in the enemy. Total casualties during this operation: 2 officers wounded. 3 O.R. killed, 14 O.R. wounded.	
	19.		All 10 guns in the line relieved by 41 & 42 M.G. Coys.	
Camp in F14 B Central Sheet 1:20.000 MONTAUBAN.	20.		Company marched to camp S.W. of MAMETZ. (F.14.B Central)	
	21st		Inspection by B.G.C. Four horses in the Brigade that took part in the Aug 18th n August 18th operations	

WAR DIARY or INTELLIGENCE SUMMARY

Army Form C. 2118.

Place	Date	Hour	Summary of Events and Information	Remarks and references to Appendices
Camp near FRICOURT	21 to 23		Rest in camp for 3 days. Company played association football against a team from 7th Bn. Grenadier Guards. Lost 0-2.	
"	24		Received orders that the 4th Army and the French would renew the attack today. 43 Bde under orders to stand to at ½ hours notice from 5.45 pm	
"	25		Orders to relieve 42 M. Gun. Co. in the line in DELVILLE WOOD. mit Coy HQ in MONTAUBAN. Advanced party under Lieut Horner. 2/Lt ANDREWS with 8 guns strikes the up camp at 9.30 pm marched to MONTAUBAN and proceeded into DELVILLE WOOD at 4.30 am 26.15.	
MONTAUBAN	26		Remainder of the 43 M.G.C. arrived about 8 am & took over. Relief complete by 10 am without casualties.	
"	27		Seven casualties in the line. Very heavy shelling. Otherwise nothing to report. Situation normal.	
"	28		Nothing to report.	
"	29		Received orders at 9pm that we will be relieved by day on the 30th by 72nd MG Coy in the line just after orders had come in notifying renewal of attack by 4th Army & French which has apparently cancelled (?) returning (?) by Wrath. Very heavy thunderstorm up to 10.30 am. At 9 signs of relieving company. Andrew men & guns	
"	30		Sent in under Lt Horner to Camp F 8. about E 18 B 6.6. CARCAILLOT FARM	

Place	Date	Hour	Summary of Events and Information	Remarks and references to Appendices
MONTAUBAN.	30 & 31	Cont.	72 M.G.Coy advanced party arrived at 7 pm - (12 hours late!) and main body at 8 pm to relieve our gun teams. They arrived at Loterm at the rendezvous and took from 5 to 6 hours crossing DELVILLE WOOD which was built unnecessary; the whole being hit. The men of 43 M.G.C. arrived back at 6 am. 74 has to march 6 miles to F8 and almost immediately on 31st DERNANCOURT a further 4 miles to entrain for ARAINES. Arrive ARAINES 9 am & had to march 10 miles to HORNOY and arrived there at 1. am. feeling very tired but thankful that the rest is near.	

31/8/16.

[signature]
Cmdg 43. M.G. Coy

To
A.G.'s Office
Machine Gun Corps Section
Base

Herewith original War Diary of the company under my command, Vol. 6 from 1/8/16 to 31/8/16

[signature] Capt.
Comdg 43rd M.G. Coy.

43RD BRIGADE MACHINE GUN COMPANY
No: MGL.160
Date: 3-9-16

To
A.A.G.
3rd Echelon.

Herewith original "War" Diary
of the company under my command
Vol.7 from 1/9/16 to 30/9/16

[signature] Capt.
cmdg 43rd M.G. Coy.

MACHINE GUN
COMPANY
MGL 190
1-10-16

Army Form C. 2118.

43. M. Gun. Co. 14
Vol. 7.

WAR DIARY
or
INTELLIGENCE SUMMARY
(Erase heading not required.)

Place	Date	Hour	Summary of Events and Information	Remarks and references to Appendices
HORNOY. 1/100,000 Sheet 16.	1st to 10th		Rest area. Company training, including Route marches, gun Drill. Range practices &c.	
	11th		Transport left by march route for AILLY/SOMME and the remainder of the Company by march route to METIGNY & took on billets there.	
MAP ALBERT 1:40,000	12		Coy augmented at 6 a.m. at ARAINES, and detrained at MERICOURT. (S14d) marched into Camp N of BERNANDCOURT.	
	13.		Nothing to report.	
	14.		Company marched with transport at 9 pm to bivouac F13C.	
	15.		Company moved up to POMMIERS Redoubt & later to MONTAUBAN S28C 8.3. About 6pm news received that 113 Inf Bde would relieve 42 W. 1 Bde in the captured enemy trenches that no section would proceed with each Bn occupying front line & one section to the supporting Bgn. When each section had reached its destination it would render	

2449 Wt. W14957/Mgo 750,000 1/16 J.B.C. & A. Forms/C.2118/12.

WAR DIARY
or
INTELLIGENCE SUMMARY
(Erase heading not required.)

Army Form C. 2118.

Place	Date	Hour	Summary of Events and Information	Remarks and references to Appendices
	15th /16		The rifles of the B.n. to which it was detailed. Orders were received later that the 43 Inf Bde would attack at 9.25 am 15th Sept the two sections accompanying the 2 B.ns (X" D.L.I & 6" Som. L.I.) detailed for the assault were instructed to follow up the infantry – advancing with the 2nd wave. The attack not being wholly successful the sections because split up & each gun was left to its leader's discretion as to what action it should take. From all accounts – there was performed (Vics Ralf Ray Wall – but are, after Cpl CRAIG, Pte's Ktout & McPHEELY the latter has slightly wounded in the head. The effective Infn 43 Bde has GIRD SUPPORT – & after the second attempt in the evening had failed – were left in action between BULLS RD and GIRD SUPPORT with 2 gunn to [supervene?] support in 9 M.Guns fire of the enemy – 5 guns in supporting positions behind – one East side of WATLING ST. by 9pm the 5 guns had withdrawn into positions in the BULLS RD north of its	[?]

WAR DIARY or INTELLIGENCE SUMMARY

Army Form C. 2118.

Place	Date	Hour	Summary of Events and Information	Remarks and references to Appendices
	16		junction with WATLING ST. when I arrived at about 8pm I found 6 guns in position in the front line & 1 in support. About 6.15pm I was detailed by the B.G.C. to take up their remaining section of 4 guns to GAP Trench & then to proceed to the front line, reconnoitre it & dispose guns as were available in depth. Accordingly I went to Bn HQ in WATLING ST. having ascertained more or less where the line was - proceeded to BULLS Rd. & sent back to GAP Trench for the guns & on their arrival placed in position & for 1 line 7 guns. 4 to the left of the line crossroad at N.32.e. Central & 3 to the right, all along BULLS Trench. East of these guns & guns were under an Officer - namely Lt. STANBURY on the left & Lt. ANDREWS with N. Sect. East Sect. has also a supporting gun placed in position about 200 yards in rear of the Castle gits group. The two guns left in GAP Trench were placed on the disposal of the N.Z.us company of the 5th Ox. Buck. L.I. & left by Lt. of the 5 TSLI respectively. During the Relating Subsequent Stay had very few targets though Hill 63 & Ploegs sport for lies - the enemy suffered severely losing 3 officers	

2449 Wt. W14957/M90 750,000 1/16 J.B.C. & A. Forms/C.2118/12.

WAR DIARY
or
INTELLIGENCE SUMMARY
(Erase heading not required.)

Army Form C. 2118.

Place	Date	Hour	Summary of Events and Information	Remarks and references to Appendices
RIBEMONT	16. 17.	}	Lt HORNER, 2Lt BORROW, & 2Lt SYERS being wounded. 3 O.R. killed. 11 O.R. missing, & 31 O.R. wounded. at 6 a.m. a relief was completed by 62 M.G. Coy. & Company marched to camp at F13C.	
	18.		Company marched at 9 a.m. to camp at RIBEMONT. Very hot & muddy.	
Rymp ALBERT	19.		Company moved into billets at RIBEMONT. & had hrs. that 14 Divn. were leave 4th ARMY & proceed by rail on 22d.	
	20.		Nothing to report. This officer re'd freemens arrived. 2Lt CAMPBELL. A & 2Lt SLOOT also 3 O.R. reinforcements	(MC)
	21.		Nothing to report. Transport left by road for SUS-ST-LEGER.	
SUS-ST-LEGER Rymp	22.		Company marched & trailer into busses by 9 a.m. & proceeded into busses via SUS-ST-LEGER. arriving there via AMIENS-DOULLENS at 2.30 pm.	
LENS.	23.		Through clean up & rest. 14th Divn. nw in 3rd Army. Received orders that 14th Divn relieves 12th Divn in the line SE of ARRAS. 43 Bde relieve 35 by Bde in H Sector. (BEAURAINS)	

Army Form C. 2118.

WAR DIARY
or
INTELLIGENCE SUMMARY
(Erase heading not required.)

Place	Date	Hour	Summary of Events and Information	Remarks and references to Appendices
"	24.		Went up to ARRAS to make arrangements, re relief of 35 M.G. Coy with transport mounted into billets at BERNEVILLE.	
	25			
ARRAS.	26.		Relieved 35 M.G. Coy in the line in H sector. SE of ARRAS. Took over 10 gun position 2L WOOD with 2L NEWTON in H or right sector with 7 guns. 2L ANDREWS with 2L ANDERSON in BONVILLE with 3 guns. (temporary)	
H Sector.	27.		Nothing to report	
	28		4 guns sent up – 2 to ATHICOURT defences under 2L SLOOT who also taken over aus. 2 two from 2L WOOD. 4 2 to BONVILLE under 2L ANDREWS.	
	29.		Improvements to various positions in the line and also 3 new higher firing positions completed.	
	30.		Night firing otherwise nothing of importance to report.	

J.A.H. Johns Captain
cmdg 42. M. Gun. Cu.

WAR DIARY

of

43RD MACHINE GUN COMPANY.

October 1st - October 31st.

Army Form C. 2118.

WAR DIARY
INTELLIGENCE SUMMARY

(Erase heading not required.) 43rd Machine Gun Company. Volume 8.

Place	Date	Hour	Summary of Events and Information	Remarks and references to Appendices
ARRAS.	Oct 1st		Nothing to report.	
	2		Altered (S4) position - to gun's crew for man firing, as present site is unsafe position.	
	3		Nothing to report.	
	4		Combined Artillery + T.M. Shoot at enemy heavy T.M's. Two Vickers guns fired 4000 rounds on high ground - supposed to be enemy O.P.	
	5th to 7th		Nothing to report. Have enemy firing with 5 guns.	
	8th		Internal relief of the Company.	
	9th 10th 12th		Nothing to report	
	13th		Shoot by Artillery + T.M. at enemy trenches and dug outs in BEAURAINS PARIT. Two Vickers guns fired 6000 rounds on camp target and V.b. fired 5000 rounds during the night. Total amount of ammunition fired during the 24 hours = 19000 rounds -	

WAR DIARY
INTELLIGENCE SUMMARY

Army Form C. 2118.

Place	Date	Hour	Summary of Events and Information	Remarks and references to Appendices
ARRAS	Oct/14 15th		Internal relief of Company. Report received from 13th D.L.I. at 12 o'clock midnight that a party of 30 Germans were laying down outside our wire at H.40. Received orders that M.G.S.O. & M.G.S.B. were to be laid on that spot, which was done, but nothing happened.	
	16 to 19		Nothing to report.	
	20		Internal relief of Company.	
	21 to 24		Except for intermine hostile artillery & T.M. fire - nothing to report	
	25		Relieved by night by 35th M. Gun. Coy. no casualties and relief completed by 10.30 pm.	
	26		Company left by bus at 7.30 pm arrived in billets at LATTRE-St-QUENTIN by 10.30 pm. Very bad billets. Transport moved by day to same place.	
LATTRE ST QUENTIN	27		Marched with transport to BEAUFORT. nil - very busy in adequate billets! No officer billets at all.	

Army Form C. 2118.

WAR DIARY
INTELLIGENCE SUMMARY
(Erase heading not required.) 43. M. Gun. Coy.

Place	Date	Hour	Summary of Events and Information	Remarks and references to Appendices
BEAUFORT	28) 29)		In Billets. Very indifferent weather. Received orders to move at 2p.m. 29th Oct. to AVERDOINGT - this order shortly after altered to 1.15 p.m. Blankets & rations were accordingly sent on, also C.Q.M.S. & Sig. Orderlies. About 12.30 p.m. (29) orders came cancelling move indefinitely; result no blankets or rations which apparently did not worry the authority who had ordered their move! Meanwhile some thirteen men neither had blankets following night.	(1)
"	30		29/30th Oct - In any army it would be worthy with 31.S. returns. Great inconvenience caused by fact of having to unloose gun limbers stands 6 miles for hands' rations. Received orders to furnish night air guard 1 Officer (Lt. SLOOT) 2 NCO's. 12 OR with 4 guns - to Grand Amm. dump AVESNES	
"	31.		Nothing to report.	

J. M. Ashton Carter
Major 43. M. Gun. Coy. 31. x. 16.

BRITISH FRONT FROM HIGH WOOD TO GINCHY.

Vol 9

Confidential
War Diary
of 43rd M.G. Coy

From 1st November 1916.　　　　To 30th November 1916

(Volume 9)

Army Form C. 2118.

WAR DIARY
or
INTELLIGENCE SUMMARY
(Erase heading not required.)

43rd Machine Gun Company
Volume 9.

Instructions regarding War Diaries and Intelligence Summaries are contained in F. S. Regs., Part II and the Staff Manual respectively. Title Pages will be prepared in manuscript.

Place	Date	Hour	Summary of Events and Information	Remarks and references to Appendices
BEAUFORT	Nov 1. 1916		Nothing to report	
	4ᵗʰ		Orders received to move to IZEL LES HAMEAU on the 6ᵗʰ.	
	5ᵗʰ		Move cancelled.	
	6ᵗʰ		Very heavy rains. Orders to move to HOUVIN on the 8ᵗʰ.	
	7ᵗʰ			
	8ᵗʰ		Marched to HOUVIN - weather stormy + raining hard. Billeting accomo.	
	9ᵗʰ		ditto cramped for the men.	
	10ᵗʰ to 30ᵗʰ		Started programme of training. Training	

J. Ward. Lieut.
Comm'g 43rd M.G. Coy.

Vol 10

War Diary.

43rd Machine Gun Company.

December 1916

Volume 10

WAR DIARY
or
INTELLIGENCE SUMMARY

(Erase heading not required.)

Army Form C. 2118.

4Post M.G. Company

Volume 10.

Place	Date	Hour	Summary of Events and Information	Remarks and references to Appendices
HOUVIN-HOUVIGNEUL	1918			
	Dec 14		Training.	
GRAND RULLECOURT	15		Marched to GRAND RULLECOURT	
WANQUETIN	16		" " WANQUETIN.	
ARRAS	17		" " ARRAS and occupied Temporary billets in the Cavalry Barracks.	
	18		Relieved the 95th M.G. Coy in 'H' Sector, putting fifteen guns into the line.	
	19			
	20		Nothing to report.	
	23			
	24		Internal relief of the Company.	
	25		Nothing to report.	
	26			
	28			
	29		Dugout at S.3. gun position, blown in by heavy trench mortar, killing two men.	

WAR DIARY
or
INTELLIGENCE SUMMARY

(Erase heading not required.)

Army Form C. 2118.

Place	Date	Hour	Summary of Events and Information	Remarks and references to Appendices
ARRAS	Dec 30 1916		Five new gun position sites and preparing for revenging the enemy's front line during raid by Durham Light Infantry.	
	31.		Work on above positions carried on.	

J.M. Dane Lt.
Comdg # 3rd R.E. Coy.

Vol XI

43rd Machine Gun Company

War Diary

January 1917

Volume II

Army Form C. 2118.

WAR DIARY
or
INTELLIGENCE SUMMARY 43rd M.G. Company
Volume II. Pages.

(Erase heading not required.)

Place	Date 1917	Hour	Summary of Events and Information	Remarks and references to Appendices
ARRAS	Jan 1	1.630	Six Guns teams left H.Q. for selected positions with carrying parties to take guns from battle positions. Raid postponed. Guns returned to manned battle position. Teams men to Coy. H.Q.	
	2	8.30	Nothing to report	
	3			
	4		ARRAS in vicinity of Coy H.Q. was shelled from 10p to 11-30p with gas & tear shells. No Company casualties.	
	5			
	6		Second company relief. Raid was carried out by D.L.I. co-operating with the 9th Division on enemy trenches N.E. of BEAURAINS. About 9pm Gun Teams left H.Q. manned the Coy. Frontline. Normally selected forward Gun Team being such that the enemy not left of the object of first. Two officers, rifles were allotted to each gun, not to open rapid fire when raiding party keeping down enemy rifle M.G. fire from his front line whilst raiding party was crossing. No them land, afterwards forming a barrage & clearing fire whilst the raiders occupied enemy trenches, finally covering their retirement to our own line. At 3.8/- all Guns opened intense fire which was maintained until 3.18pm when the raiding party left our front line & moved to the enemy's trenches. From then onwards until 3.50pm a steady fire was maintained on the	

Army Form C. 2118.

WAR DIARY or INTELLIGENCE SUMMARY
(Erase heading not required.)

Place	Date	Hour	Summary of Events and Information	Remarks and references to Appendices
ARRAS	June 6 (continued)		enemies of the raid. French was the Officer in charge for return Guns not observed intense fire was re-opened on original targets. At 4.30 p.m. all guns ceased fire. During the raid 29,000 rounds of S.A.A. were fired & no casualties occurred in the Company. Guns were afterwards returned to their battle position. Teams to Company H.Q.	
	7 to 10		Very quiet & nothing to report. Guns fired as usual at their night targets about 10,000 rounds per night being fired	
	11		Pre. Savino Pte. BONVILLE sub-sector were relieved by 4th M.G. Squadron, which would enable the remaining men (approximately) manned by the company to have a complete relief every 2nd day. Internal Company relief also took place this day without casualties	
	12 to 16		Quiet. Owing to bad weather & trenches in need of repair. Parties of 20 men worked on them each day considerably improving their condition. Usual night firing from about to dawn each night without casualties	
	17 18		Internal relief of Company without casualties. Heavy full Honors. Quiet.	

WAR DIARY
or
INTELLIGENCE SUMMARY

Army Form C. 2118.

Place	Date 1917	Hour	Summary of Events and Information	Remarks and references to Appendices
ARRAS	Jan 19		Situation general. Working party of 20 men in 3 shifts building new dugout.	
	20		Men employment employed in RONVILLE Sub-sector support line.	
	21		4 guns teams temporary relieved in H.S. Sub-sector by 4th M.G. Squadron. About 5pm Considerable portion of H. Sub-sector support line blown in by enemy trench mortars, communication trench leading to one of the M.G. positions was completely blocked. Working party of 15 men left Coy. H.Q. at 10pm to repair the trench returned by 3.30am. No company casualties.	
	22		Nothing to report. Usual working parties night firing. Enemy trench mortars active.	
	23		Nothing to report. Exceptionally hard frost for several days.	
	24		1 Officer reinforcement joined.	
	25		Daylight M.G. Sniping position in course of construction in a house at RONVILLE. For the purpose of snipers at enemy sentries re. wiring land working parties on new dugout. Frequently been observed by late Observing & Strengthen Old dugouts repairing trench. Night firing as usual. 10 O.R. reinforcement arrived	

WAR DIARY
or
INTELLIGENCE SUMMARY

Army Form C. 2118.

Place	Date 1917	Hour	Summary of Events and Information	Remarks and references to Appendices
ARRAS	Jan 26		Enemy Trench mortars exceedingly active, several dropping near M.G. positions without damage. Day light Sniping practice completed, patrol up this position of the enemy who were observed to leave their trenches, were dispersed each by a short burst, leaving to dwell on the arms. 24 men attached from Battalion in the Brigade, to be trained as snipers.	
	27		Company relieved 4th M.G. Squadron on H1 & RONVILLE Subsectors at 10 am. This Essential. Re-company is now manning 14 gun positions, also 1 team proceeds daily to sniping post. No enemy Snipers were observed from to latter during the 27th. Silence still continue necessitating the use of rifle fire at night-time in order to prevent fire from freezing.	
	28 to 30		Schuster quiet. Enemy trench mortar of particularly active on 30th done Enemy gun positions but without damage, also considerable falling very near gun positions but no fire from enemy's trench or dug outs. Our constant M.G. night firing on our various lines of approach has been effective as he has now lost another line of tramways to be abandoned. The new line is now being dealt with.	
	31		Nothing particular to report.	

M. Land. Capt.
O.C. 3rd M.G. Coy.

No 12

War Diary

43rd Machine Gun Company

Volume 12

February 1917

Army Form C. 2118.

WAR DIARY
or
INTELLIGENCE SUMMARY

(Erase heading not required.)

431. M.G.Coy.

Volume 12. Page 1.

Instructions regarding War Diaries and Intelligence Summaries are contained in F. S. Regs., Part II. and the Staff Manual respectively. Title Pages will be prepared in manuscript.

Place	Date 1917	Hour	Summary of Events and Information	Remarks and references to Appendices
ARRAS.	Feb. 1.		Large new position dugout now completed by Special party working with M/c R.E's. Enemy shows signs of annoyance at our night M.G. fire on his rear track tramway, by searching for our position with his M.Gs. Internal relief of H1. RONVILLE Sector. No casualties.	
	2.			
	3 to 6	}	Nothing to report. Usual night firing.	
	7.		New gun position in ACHICOURT Sub-Sector relieved by 21st. M.G.Coy. No casualties. Enemy active with larger calibre shells than usual.	
	8.		Five Gun positions in RONVILLE Sub-sector and one in H1 Sub-sector relieved by 42 M.G.Coy. Also 3 positions in AGNY Sub-sector taken over from 42 M.G.Coy. These reliefs have considerably lessened the Brigade front covered by guns of this company, tho' all guns which fire over this front are retained, including night firing lines.	
	9.		Internal relief remaining H1 sub-sector. No casualties. ACHICOURT guns manned by this company are re-arranged from this date. These gun positions known as RIGHT & LEFT Sectors, each containing 4 guns.	

WAR DIARY or INTELLIGENCE SUMMARY

Army Form C. 2118.

Page 2

Place	Date	Hour	Summary of Events and Information	Remarks and references to Appendices
ARRAS	Feb 9 (cont)		Each Sect'n is under the command of 1 Officer. In addition two night firing lines in front of the 43rd Bde. Sects trl covering it are manned each night — controlled from Coy. HQ. No casualties have occurred during these re-distributing reliefs which have been carried out by day. Working party of 20 men supplied K.R.E's from 3p.m. to 10 p.m.	
	10		Working party of 10 men supplied by R.E. from 3am to 6am. Stretcher Quick Class held daily for training of orderlies (men attached from Battalion). Guns fire on average of 5000 rounds per night on enemy trenches, roads &c.	
	11 to 14		Nothing to report. Working parties of 30 men per day under Pioneers. Classes & night firing continues.	
	15 16 to 20		External Company relief. No casualties. Daily working parties supplied to R.E.'s. Trench revetted, deepened & cleared, new aeroplane emplacement constructed by teams in line. Fresh firing as usual. Training of attached men at H.Q. 5 O.R. reinforcements arrived 18-2-17. 2 Officers admitted to Hospital.	

WAR DIARY
or
INTELLIGENCE SUMMARY Page 3

Army Form C. 2118.

Place	Date 1917	Hour	Summary of Events and Information	Remarks and references to Appendices
ARRAS	Feb.	21	Internal Relief of Company. No casualties.	
		22 & 23	Working parties, repairs to trenches - deepening, revetting, manual might firing, classes training continued	
		24	Company H.Q. changed billets	
		25 to 28	Situation normal. Anti-aircraft aircraft mountings erected at Trench Company H.Q. Internal relief of Company on 27th. No casualties. Working parties under R.E.'s, classes &c. &c. continued.	

Maur Capt
Cmdg 43 M.G. Coy

Vol.13

CONFIDENTIAL.

WAR   DIARY.
****

43rd Machine Gun Company.
****

For month of March 1917.
****

Volume. 13.
****

Army Form C. 2118.

43rd. M.G. Company.

WAR DIARY
or
INTELLIGENCE SUMMARY

(Erase heading not required.)

Volume 13. Page 1.

Instructions regarding War Diaries and Intelligence Summaries are contained in F. S. Regs., Part II. and the Staff Manual respectively. Title Pages will be prepared in manuscript.

Place	Date	Hour	Summary of Events and Information	Remarks and references to Appendices
ARRAS.	1917 March 1.		at Coy.H.Q. M.G. mounted for Anti-aircraft used against hostile aeroplanes over Arras.	
		2	Range built at H.Q. for Classes. Firing Course. Usual working parties. Night firing re. Re-inoculation of men who have not been inoculated for 12 months commenced.	
		3	Four extra M.G. positions taken over from 42nd M.G.Coy.	
		4	Nothing to report.	
		5	Internal Company relief. Working parties most REs discontinued. Night working parties revetting sleeping trenches. Daylight Coyprn position manned each day from Coy. H.Q.	
		6 to 9	Four special positions under construction for raid purposes. Night firing on Gyps on enemy's wire points behind his line. Working parties revetting & deepening sleeping trenches.	
		10	Raid on enemy's trenches postponed. Night firing on Gyps an wire maintained. 12 men at present in Hospital sick.	
		11.	1 O.R. evacuated. Internal Company relief. Enemy shelled ARRAS intermittently	

WAR DIARY or INTELLIGENCE SUMMARY

Army Form C. 2118.

Page 2.

Place	Date	Hour	Summary of Events and Information	Remarks and references to Appendices
ARRAS	1917 March 12.	All day.	Raid by 8th ROY.L.I on enemy trenches took place at 7pm. 43 M.G.Coy. assisted with four guns — two barraging each flank & raided assisted with an attacking position for front. Some difficulty was experienced in obtaining position for these guns as the target in each case was very close to its raiding party thereby necessitating direct laying. Essentially two guns were placed in the top of a house in RENVILLE & two more being situated in another house fired through the roof. Ranges of four guns averaged 1100 yds. nearer the line. The two 600-900 yd. positions were not considered ideal but were the best that could be obtained to meet the requirements. Shrapnel proof covered emplacements were constructed in each case. Each pair of guns were under the control of an Officer. Fire was opened at zero rate intense for eight minutes, after which barrage fire of 250 rounds per 4 minutes was maintained for 22 minutes. Fire ceased for ½ minute then opened intense again for 8 minutes, ceased after another	

WAR DIARY or INTELLIGENCE SUMMARY

Army Form C. 2118.

Place	Date 1917	Hour	Summary of Events and Information	Remarks and references to Appendices
ARRAS.	Mar. 13		10 minute barrage fire. A direct hit dislodged airplane portion at trench H.Q. Maypole. During the raid a gunner of the left gun observed a party of 30-40 Germans on a ridge of front a hill at them causing casualties. A little retaliation fire was heard but not directed towards M.G. position. At the end of the raid the Moving Supporters on D the right gun collapsed & orders to the bottom of the hollow. Shelling of the gun team fell to the bottom of the hollow. One of the gun team only was injured to the team. Most fortunately enemy located by the enemy. Total company casualties – 1 O.R. wounded 2 O.R. wounded (remained at duty). 21,750 rounds S.A.A. were fired.	
	14.		Situation normal. Intermittent shelling of ARRAS. Night firing continued. Eight gun position on Hr. Gutscotor taken over by 169 M.G. Coy. Relief carried out in daylight without casualties. 43 M.G. Coy moves into	
	15} 16} 16}		Mans Juin position in RONVILLE Sub sector. 14 men in hospital sick. Enemy searched for gun position (night firing) unit 5.9's. Considerable work done in repairing, deepening revetting, trenches.	

WAR DIARY or INTELLIGENCE SUMMARY

Army Form C. 2118.

Page 4.

Place	Date 1917	Hour	Summary of Events and Information	Remarks and references to Appendices
ARRAS	March 17. 18.		Infernal company relief Brigade sector evacuated, also BEAURAINS. Enemy line opposite occupied. Infantry patrol pushed forward established behind enemy's front line system 4 guns under 1 Officer & 1 Sgt. (teams of 4 men, 1N.C.O. & 4 carriers) sent up to cover front flanks. The four guns remained at their stations. Occupying positions behind our line remained on line.	
	19.		Present front line now faces TILLOY and strong point known as The Harp, being about 1000 to 1200 yds away. Considerable shelling of trenches by night but daytime is fairly quiet. M.G.'s were fired on parties of enemy observed on TELEGRAPH HILL dispersing them. One M.G. moved up from support to front line on right flank. 17 PREUSEN WEG leaving 2 guns in support & 2 guns in front line	
	20		Enemy again shelled trenches at night but morning was quiet. Four advanced guns relieved slowly afternoon sections. Canadian H.Q's moved forward to dug-out in original support line	

Army Form C. 2118.

WAR DIARY
or
INTELLIGENCE SUMMARY

(Erase heading not required.)

Page 5.

Place	Date 1917	Hour	Summary of Events and Information	Remarks and references to Appendices
EAST OF ARRAS.	March 21.		Another noisy night, enemy shelling scattered fire. Apparently areas in TILLOY WOOD are kept used as O.Ps by enemy as his Vickers & his Lewis guns spend fire on same from front line but the only apparent result was to cause these guns to be shelled. They accurately ceased fire but when his guns from reserve were brought into action attack fell on M5b (Central) (Sh 51 t SW1) fired on same target with little effect.	
		22.	Rather ineffective enemy artillery fire during night coupled with M.G. fire traversing our front line. Two M.G.s of the Company fired on trees in TILLOY as previously during his time. During 23rd our Right gun fired on enemy convoy observed on TILLOY-NEUVILLE-VITASSE Road. The men leaving their carts for shelter. Intermittent heavy hostile fire, several thinks fury reported. 8 O.R. reinforcements arrived.	
		24.	4/01 M.G.Coy. relieved 4 advanced guns & 4 reserve guns in RONVILLE without casualties	
ARRAS		25.	Whole Company billeted in ARRAS. 2 Officer reinforcements arrived	

WAR DIARY
or
INTELLIGENCE SUMMARY

Page 6

Army Form C. 2118.

Place	Date 1917	Hour	Summary of Events and Information	Remarks and references to Appendices
ARRAS	March 26.		Company moved to DAINVILLE for training	
DAINVILLE	27 to 31.		Detailed training for offensive, open fighting, carried out	

M.Sims Capt
O.C. 243 M.G. Coy.

WAR DIARY

43rd Machine Gun Company
/14
Volume 14

April 1917.

WAR DIARY
or
INTELLIGENCE SUMMARY

Army Form C. 2118.

43rd M.G. Company
Volume 14. Page 1.

Place	Date 1917	Hour	Summary of Events and Information	Remarks and references to Appendices
DAINVILLE	April 1.		Advanced training – Harassing open fighting	
	2.		Company moved to ARRAS. 2 Sections of Company moved to ARRAS & proceeded into line with 8 guns (4 in line 4 in reserve) relieving 41/91 M.G. Coy.	
	3.		1 Section of Company sent to Corps Depot Camp FOSSEUX H.Q. moved into ARRAS in evening. 1 Section left at DAINVILLE for training. Vicinity of H.Q. intermittently shelled, one shell killing 1 O.R.	
	4.		1 Officer reinforcement arrived.	
	5.		1 Gun destroyed by shellfire - direct hit. No casualties. Team in reserve relieved team in trench which latter proceeded to reserve.	
	6.		Nothing to report.	
	7.		Teams in line relieved. Reserve team withdrawn to Coy. H.Q. No 2 Section proceeded with guns from DAINVILLE to ARRAS.	
	8.		Reserve Guns & barrage guns carried to forward positions. At 5.15a No 2 Section proceeded to assembly trenches with guns. No 1 & 4 Sections occupied position for purpose of barrage fire. Company H.Q. moved	

WAR DIARY or INTELLIGENCE SUMMARY

Army Form C. 2118.

Page 2

Place	Date 1917	Hour	Summary of Events and Information	Remarks and references to Appendices
ARRAS	April	8. (cont)	to advanced position. Advanced Transport camp situated at ARRAS.	
		9.	ZERO hour fixed for 5.30am. Four guns were detailed for covering fire. Four guns were kept in reserve in a dugout nearby. Eight guns for Barrage fire was apparently effective as several dead Germans were afterwards found killed by long range M.G. bullets. At ZERO - 2 hrs 4 mins attacking troops moved forward. The 4 guns detailed to accompany them followed with 4th wave moving to within 100 yds 1st objective waiting under cover until infantry were established when they occupied position during the advance to second objective. No firing was carried out. 4 guns moved up to the 1st line. When infantry had occupied rail & some effective shooting on targets which presented themselves. Immediately the second objective was captured four more guns were sent to reinforce guns already established there. A third section of 4 guns was moved up to 1st objective. Two guns moved forward with several L.I. to attack third objective. The remaining guns in second objective carrying out covering fire on trenches in front of WANCOURT also on some high ground on Right flank. They engaged several parties of enemy infantry. This advance was silenced.	

Place	Date	Hour	Summary of Events and Information	Remarks and references to Appendices
E. of ARRAS	1917 April 9		Not much further than WANCOURT-TILLOY Rd. All the days fighting was carried out under intermittent rain & snow storms.	
	10		The Durham L.I. & R.O.Y.L.I. were detailed to capture the third objective & another 2 guns were sent up to join the two already forward. The whole section of 4 guns to move behind the infantry. The section in second objective were also placed forward to positions covering right flank. The guns obtained many targets including a M.G. Rifleman many casualties on the enemy. The third objective was captured & the four guns established in the first objective being moved in the line the section on the WANCOURT-TILLOY Rd. forward into support on a specially made trg. resembling a During this advance the 4 guns were used to carry the guns Perpendicular on the middle of the tracks & was found most effective in concealing the guns. Whole company were relieved on evening of 10th. by 410 M.G. Coy. & proceeded to Caves in RONVILLE. At 8 p.m. orders were received that Division would be relieved	

WAR DIARY or INTELLIGENCE SUMMARY

Army Form C. 2118.

Page 4.

Place	Date 1917	Hour	Summary of Events and Information	Remarks and references to Appendices
ARRAS	April 11 (cont)	9	43 M.G.Coy. moved into ARRAS staying in billets the night.	
	12		Company moved to AGNEZ-LES-DUISANS.	
	13		" " GIVENCHY-LE-NOBLE	
	14		" " SUS-ST-LEGER	
SUS ST LEGER	15 to 22		Training, re-equipping, sports &c.	
			8 O.R. reinforcements arrived 18.4.17	
			1 Officer " " 19.4.17.	
	23		Orders received for move to SAULTY area. Move cancelled 5pm. 1 Schn.	
			proceeded to SAULTY mounting antiaircraft guns over dumps.	
BASSEUX	24		Company moved to BASSEUX.	
	25 26		} Nothing to report	
	27		Company less 3 Officers 25 men who proceeded to reinforcements	
			Camp at MONCHIET, marched to RONVILLE.	
RONVILLE	28 to 30		Company in reserve at RONVILLE. 18 O.R. in Hospital. Two guns with personnel 3 Officers 4 men placed under C.R.A. for artillery defensive barrage at HENINEL.	

M.Evans Capt.
cmdg. 43 M.G.Coy.

Vol 15

WAR   DIARY.

For month of M A Y 1917.

43rd Machine Gun Company.

Volume. 15.

Army Form C. 2118.

WAR DIARY or INTELLIGENCE SUMMARY

43rd M.G. Company
Volume 15. Page 1.

(Erase heading not required.)

Place	Date 1917	Hour	Summary of Events and Information	Remarks and references to Appendices
RONVILLE	May 1.		Nothing to report. Limbers packed with S.A.A carts ready for immediate use.	
		2.	Company Transport marched to position about 1000 yds N.W. of WANCOURT. Some shells dropped in vicinity of camp during night.	
		3.	Company stood to at 3.30am in reserve with 43 Inf. Bde. to 41st and 42nd Inf. Bdes. During the early part of morning enemy shells, apparently intended for Batteries situated on other side of this camp, burst in the Transport lines near position occupied by Company Transport. No Casualties (humans) also two Animal casualties. Transport was moved some distance west together with the whole of Brigade Transport. ~~who spent time together with brigade transport~~ During the day Transport lines were again moved to a less conspicuous position. Company remained "standing to".	
WANCOURT			During afternoon 3rd. 2 Guns under an Officer reinforced 41st M.G.Coy.	
		4.	Company remained in reserve until night of 4th-5th. when it moved into the line east of WANCOURT taking over the whole Divisional front covered by 41st & 42nd M.G.Coys.	
IN the Line		5 to 9	During this period the whole front was subjected to heavy enemy	

WAR DIARY
or
INTELLIGENCE SUMMARY Volume 15. Page 2.

Army Form C. 2118.

Place	Date	Hour	Summary of Events and Information	Remarks and references to Appendices
EAST OF WANCOURT	1917 May 7	5 to 9	Artillery fire large calibre. No important operation took place but the following minor events are recorded. On the morning of 7th the right flank of division on left were to occupy the trench in front of them by a "trickling forward" movement. Guns of the company were to cover their operation by firing on targets opposite themselves on the outskirts of BOIS DU VERT. A few parties of the enemy were observed running at once causing six or seven casualties. On the 8th the teams in one section from the direction of CHERISY. This was promptly replied to by return enemy and their rifles. Some teams interfered with enemy coming from the direction of CHERISY. This was promptly replied to by return enfilade with M.Guns and remainder of teams used their rifles. Some shelling being observed. During the 9th information was received, was borne out by aeroplane photograph, that the enemy was using infantry tracks east of TRIANGLE WOOD. Our shelling have been effective on the roads in this neighborhood but leaving this particular spot almost untouched. Guns fired indirectly on these paths during the night using 1700 rounds, were apparently effective as the enemy heavily retaliated with M.Gs artillery searching	

Army Form C. 2118.

WAR DIARY
or
INTELLIGENCE SUMMARY

(Erase heading not required.)

Volume 15. Page 3.

Place	Date 1917	Hour	Summary of Events and Information	Remarks and references to Appendices
EAST VANCOURT.	May	5	for our guns unsuccessfully but caused some casualties to infantry in the vicinity.	
		15	During these days troops in the line had to endure a very strenuous time. The trenches being often reduced ratherthin from continuous severe heavy Barrage fire were frequently indulged in rather concentrated bombardments blackened scattered fire over large areas accounted for not a few casualties.	
		9		
		10	On the afternoon of 10th the 43 Inf. Bde. took over 500 additional yards of front from 53 Inf. Bde., on its right. This necessitated bending forward 3 guns into the new area to occupy positions vacated by 53 M.G. Coy. 13 guns were now in the line. 2 guns with 47 Bde. R.F.A. on Artillery defence work & 1 gun was under repair being damaged by shell fire.	
		6	To support an attack by 168 Inf. Bde. (43 Bde. left flank) on CAVALRY FARM and TOE TRENCH — which ran north from the farm — 6 guns were moved on night 10/11. Hand gears to	
		14	sweep COJEUL VALLEY & place a barrage fire on area behind	

2449 Wt. W14957/M90 750,000 1/16 J.B.C. &A. Forms/C.2118/12.

Army Form C. 2118.

WAR DIARY
or
INTELLIGENCE SUMMARY

(Erase heading not required.)

Volume 15. Page 4.

Place	Date 1917	Hour	Summary of Events and Information	Remarks and references to Appendices
EAST OF MONCHY	May 10 to 14th.		TOOL TRENCH. The position was however carried through overnight by 168 Bde. without the intervention of our guns, which remained in their position on night of 10/11. in anticipation of a counter-attack which did not materialise. The heavy hostile artillery fire of previous days was continued intermittently over the whole period. Very little relief was received by our own artillery. The Company was relieved by 41st Coy. on night of 14/15th. The relief being effected without casualties to all ranks. The period 4th - 14th May was a very severe trial to all ranks. The teams having to live in the open trenches. Heavy enemy artillery throughout the whole period which applied artillery bombardment which was particularly trying at night to teams returning ration parties. The company sustained a thorough? A notable feature was "intermittent shelling" of our rear area by the enemy with long range and 5 killed in casualties, naval guns which caused transport dumps to seek new positions on more than one occasion.	
BEAURAINS		15 to 25	In Divisional Reserve near BEAURAINS. Training, & sports programmes carried on. 2 gun teams advanced with RFA. On evening of 25th. 1 Company moved to Support Area N. of NEUVILLE VITASSE	

Army Form C. 2118.

WAR DIARY
or
INTELLIGENCE SUMMARY

(Erase heading not required.)

Volume 15. Page 5.

Instructions regarding War Diaries and Intelligence Summaries are contained in F.S. Regs., Part II. and the Staff Manual respectively. Title Pages will be prepared in manuscript.

Place	Date 1917	Hour	Summary of Events and Information	Remarks and references to Appendices
N.J. NEUVILLE VITASSE	May 25		Relieving 42nd M.G.Coy. Company in support. 3 Guns Teams under an Officer occupied Company defensive positions at WANCOURT.	
	26		Nothing to report.	
	27		Brigade drill Competition took place when M.G. Transport won a first prize for turnout & Teams	
	28		Left Guns Competition proceeded to trenches to take part in a chased Divisional Machine Gun effort against hostile aeroplanes which had been flying low over our lines in the early morning.	
	29			
	30 & 31		Hostile aircraft did not fly over our own trenches these mornings & Guns had an opportunity of opening fire. They were withdrawn on evening 31st, when the 3 support Guns at WANCOURT were also relieved by fresh Teams of the Company.	

Mourn Capt
Comdg 43 M.G.Coy.

Vol 16

War Diary

43rd Machine Gun Company

JUNE 1917

Volume 16

Army Form C. 2118.

WAR DIARY
or
INTELLIGENCE SUMMARY

(Erase heading not required.)

43rd M.G. Coy.

Volume 16. Page 1.

Instructions regarding War Diaries and Intelligence Summaries are contained in F. S. Regs., Part II. and the Staff Manual respectively. Title Pages will be prepared in manuscript.

Place	Date	Hour	Summary of Events and Information	Remarks and references to Appendices
N. of NEUVILLE VITASSE	June 1917 1		Company relieved in Support Area. 2 O.R. casualties caused by gas shells whilst carrying guns to line for anti-aircraft work.	
E. of HANCOURT		2.	43 M.G. Coy relieved 42 M.G. Coy on the line taking over 11 Gun positions.	
		3.	Situation quiet. Enemy aeroplanes flew over our lines at night and early morning.	
		4.	Hostile aircraft again active at night. Enemy used Tear shells about 9.30 p.m. 1 O.R. gassed by Gas shells when on carrying party.	
		5.	Nothing to report.	
		6.	Three Guns specially detailed for anti-aircraft work to deal with enemy activity in morning & evening. Also 2 defensive Guns similarly employed during day time.	
		7.	Quiet. Guns detailed fired at enemy aeroplanes attempting to fly over our lines at low altitude.	
		8.	Three anti-aircraft guns withdrawn	
		9.	Nothing to report.	
		10.	2 Guns with 47th Bde. R.F.A. for defensive work, aircraft work relieved by 53 M.G. Coy. Set Guns on right sector relieved on night 10-11th by 169 M.G. Coy and 193 M.G. Coy.	

WAR DIARY or INTELLIGENCE SUMMARY

Army Form C. 2118.

Volume 16. Page 2.

Place	Date 1917	Hour	Summary of Events and Information	Remarks and references to Appendices
	June	11	During the day details camp moved to Reserve Bde. Camp near BEAURAINS. Remaining 5 Guns in line on Regtl Sector relieved at night by 53rd M.G. Coy & teams marched back to BEAURAINS.	
BEAURAINS	-	12	Guns cleaned. Limbers packed ready for move	
BEAUMETZ	-	13	Company marched to BEAUMETZ	
GAUDIEMPRE	-	14	" " " GAUDIEMPRE	
AUTHIE	-	15	" " " AUTHIE	
-	-	16	Commenced training	
-	-	17	Training	
	-	25	"	
	-	26	14th Divisional Horse Show - Company took 1st prize for pack animal and 2nd for Turnout of a limbered wagon & pair	
	-	27	An escaped German prisoner - Sgt Major BRAUN was captured in LALEAU WOOD by a search party of the company.	
	-	30	Training continued.	

J. Ward Capt.
Comg 43rd M.G. Coy

Vol 17

Confidential

War Diary

of

43rd Machine Gun Company

From July 1st 1917   To July: 31st 1917

(Vol. 17)

O/C
43 Inf Bde.

Herewith War Diary Volume
17 of the Company under
my Command, from
1/7/17 — 31/7/17

H W Baggs 2/Lt for Capt

Cmdg 43 M.G. Coy.

43RD
MACHINE GUN
COMPANY.
No. ER 35
Date 1.8.17

Army Form C. 2118.

WAR DIARY
or
INTELLIGENCE SUMMARY

43 MG Company

Volume 17

(Erase heading not required.)

Instructions regarding War Diaries and Intelligence Summaries are contained in F. S. Regs., Part II. and the Staff Manual respectively. Title Pages will be prepared in manuscript.

Place	Date 1917	Hour	Summary of Events and Information	Remarks and references to Appendices
AUTHIE	July 1 to 9		Training programme carried out	
GEZAINCOURT	10		Company marched to GEZAINCOURT	
	11		Entrained at DOULLENS about 5 pm	
BAILLEUL	12		Detrained at BAILLEUL midnight. Marched to CROIX de POPERINGHE north of BAILLEUL arrived about 2:30 am	
CROIX de POPERINGHE	13 to		Training	
	14		1 Officer 20 O.R. detached for defence of dumps from hostile aircraft at DRANOUTRE.	
	15			
	16 to 25		Training	
	26		Inspection by Army Commander	
	27		Anti-aircraft detachment at DRANOUTRE relieved by 249 M.G. Coy.	
	28 to 31		Training . on 27th.	

Meurs Capt.
OC 43 M.G. Coy.

Vol 18

WAR DIARY

43rd Machine Gun Company
14

AUGUST 1917

Volume 18

Army Form C. 2118.

WAR DIARY
or
INTELLIGENCE SUMMARY

43rd M.G. Coy
Volume 16

(Erase heading not required.)

Instructions regarding War Diaries and Intelligence
Summaries are contained in F. S. Regs., Part II.
and the Staff Manual respectively. Title Pages
will be prepared in manuscript.

Place	Date 1917	Hour	Summary of Events and Information	Remarks and references to Appendices
CROIX de POPERINGHE	Aug 1. to 5.		Training, special feature being made of M.G. barrage fire. 1 O.R. evacuated, 1 O.R. reinforcement.	
CAESTRE	6		Company marched to billet N.W. of CAESTRE.	
	7.		1 O.R. evacuated. 1 O.R. reinforcement	
	8		Inspection by D.G.C.	
	9 to 14		Training	
NW ABEELE	15.		Marched to billet N.W. of ABEELE	
	16		Training	
	17		Marched to OUDERDOM. After half of 2 hours camp was changed. Marched to N. of DICKEBUSCH.	
N. DICKEBUSCH	18 & 19		In camp N. of DICKEBUSCH.	
	20		In the evening company relieved 41st M.G. Coy. in trenches E. of HOOGE. 2 O.R. wounded.	

WAR DIARY or INTELLIGENCE SUMMARY

Page 2

Place	Date	Hour	Summary of Events and Information	Remarks and references to Appendices
E. of HOOGE	Aug. 21 1917		Nothing special to report. 2 O.R. wounded	
	22 and 23		16 Guns in the line – 8 defensive, 6 to assist in smoke/stokes? operations & exploited trenches & 2 in reserve, which latter were required to replace casualties. Before zero hour at 7am, 22nd, the infantry attacked INVERNESS COPSE. 2 Guns were attacked to Left Battalion, 2 to Right Battalion & 2 to Battalion supporting right flank. The guns attacked to Left Battalion assembled in shell holes moved forward behind the 1st wave of infantry. As the rest of the infantry were held up by machine gun fire the Officer i/c B machine guns got into action, knocked out an enemy machine gun & dispersed a bombing party, whereupon the infantry were able to advance & consolidate. In the meantime the two machine guns engaged many targets with good effect. They were then moved to a position where they commanded the area between GLENCROSS WOOD and INVERNESS COPSE who had flanking fire both ways. On the following day, 23rd, they fired in response to our "S.O.S." signal & also knocked out a troublesome mobile machine gun at L shaped farm. The 2 guns attacked to the Right Battalion moved forward on morning of the attack & took up position in INVERNESS COPSE on either flank. The right gun engaged several targets but owing to the arrival of infantry Reinforcements in the general confusion, it was left unattended	

Army Form C. 2118.

WAR DIARY
or
INTELLIGENCE SUMMARY
(Erase heading not required.)

Page 3

Place	Date 1917	Hour	Summary of Events and Information	Remarks and references to Appendices
E. of HOOGE	Aug 22 & 23 (Continued)		About 50 yards in front of our infantry. In the early morning of the 23rd a strong hostile party appeared within 20 yards of the gun. The N.C.O. in charge attempted to get it away but was obliged to leave it, one of his men being killed. Later he crawled out and secured the gun & some ammunition, making three journeys in all. A battalion was detailed to form a defensive flank on the right, but the 2 guns attached to it suffered heavy casualties from the enemy barrage, which dropped immediately on the French they occupied. Lost 75% of personnel of one gun. The other gun was crawled out into "No Mans Land" & escaped further shelling. Another gun team was sent up to reinforce. These guns were troubled by snipers from beyond S. of INVERNESS COPSE, but in spite of this obtained many targets including a party of 20-30 men, of which only 4 were seen to escape. Enemy guns were all able to fire where they did good work only 2 of the defensive guns being held by the enemy. Casualties 22nd & 23rd — 8 O.R. killed, 1 Off. missing, 1 Officer wounded, 21 O.R. wounded.	
	24th		During the night 23-24th enemy heavily shelled front line & rear down. The "S.O.S." was sent up but little movement could be seen & 15 minutes later the infantry liquid fire being observed in INVERNESS COPSE	

Army Form C. 2118.

WAR DIARY
or
INTELLIGENCE SUMMARY
(Erase heading not required.)

Page 4

Place	Date	Hour	Summary of Events and Information	Remarks and references to Appendices
E of HOOGE	Aug 24 (cont.)		At the same time 4 Machine Guns opened fire upon hostile sights & succeeded with rifle fire in preventing any further advance of the enemy, who were in large numbers. At 4.50 am the left gun of two knocked out by a shell the infantry on left flank had to fall back withdrew then advanced again & recaptured their original position. During the rest of the day many targets were fired on with visible effect. Concentrations of the enemy were dispersed & hostile machine guns silenced by combined shooting of our remaining three machine guns. In the afternoon about 3.30 pm the enemy were seen massing about 200–300 strong towards FITZ CLARENCE FARM. The machine guns were trained on this point no further movement was observed. During the evening the enemy were seen in two & threes crawling up towards the hedges & were sniped with bursts of fire. Of the two guns in INVERNESS COPSE one was surrounded on three sides shortly after the sergeant in charge had got it out & action by firing his revolver into it. Only one man from this team survived. In the night fire nothing has been heard. On the right flank were two guns who were under a heavy bombardment all night, at dawn the enemy were advancing from the copse & the left gun was surrounded & routed. The gunners returned at their posts & fired continuously until the No. 1	

Army Form C. 2118.

WAR DIARY or INTELLIGENCE SUMMARY

Page 5

Place	Date	Hour	Summary of Events and Information	Remarks and references to Appendices
Esquelbecq	Aug 24 (cont)		was wounded in the eye. The Officer in charge of another man were taken prisoner, but managed to get away in our barrage coming down. The right gun was withdrawn into our front line just into action with good effect. The infantry were forced back to our old line shortly & the gun was ordered back by an infantry officer. It got into action again on reinforcing parties of the enemy coming over the ridge. A counter attack regained the crest edge of the copse. Another gun was sent up to reinforce the right flank. The defensive guns suffered severely from shell fire but all remaining guns fired. They were reinforced by 2 guns from 249 M.G.Coy — one being used on the right flank. One in a forward corner. The north edge of the wood. During the day about 10,000 rounds per gun were fired by the front line guns. The infantry assisted in filling belts, ammunition being collected from trenchers taken off casualties. A supply of 5,000 boxes were sent up in addition making a reserve of about 8,000 rounds per gun. Owing to the closeness of many tables by the targets the enemy undoubtedly suffered heavy losses. Casualties 24th — 7 OR killed, 3 OR missing, 16 OR wounded. Total casualties for the period: — 15 OR killed, 4 OR missing, 1 Officer wounded, 41 OR wounded	

Army Form C. 2118.

WAR DIARY
or
INTELLIGENCE SUMMARY

Page 6

(Erase heading not required.)

Instructions regarding War Diaries and Intelligence Summaries are contained in F. S. Regs., Part II. and the Staff Manual respectively. Title Pages will be prepared in manuscript.

Place	Date 1917	Hour	Summary of Events and Information	Remarks and references to Appendices
E. of HOOGE	Aug 24 (about)		Rear mobile men attached no carriers.	
OUDERDOM	25.		Company who relieved by 41st M.G. Coy. Marched to camp N.W. of OUDERDOM	
	26 to 28		Camp at OUDERDOM.	
	29		Marched to camp in ROUKLOSHILLE Area.	
	30 to 31		Camp at ROUKLOSHILLE Area.	

J. Maud Capt.
Cmdg 43 M.G. Coy.

WAR DIARY.

43rd Machine Gun Company.

September 1917.

Volume. 19.

Army Form C. 2118.

WAR DIARY
or
INTELLIGENCE SUMMARY 43 M.G. Company
Volume 19
(Erase heading not required.)

Place	Date	Hour	Summary of Events and Information	Remarks and references to Appendices
ROUKLOSHILLE Area	Sept. 1		83 O.R. reinforcements arrived night 31st August.	
	2, 3		Nothing to report	
	4		Company marched to camp E. of STEENWERCK.	
E. of STEENWERCK	5 to 14		Training	
NEUVE EGLISE	15		Company marched to NEUVE EGLISE.	
	16 to 18		Training	
	19		Battery of 6 in. Guns for barrage attached to 41st M.G. Coy. for next operation for many of Bgd.	
	20		Company relieved 41st M.G. Coy. in line taking over 11 Gun positions.	
E. of MESSINES	21 to 23		Nothing special to report. Enemy shelling heavy in parts - considerable aerial activity. 6 Casualties (wounded) during the period	

2449 Wt. W14957/M90. 750,000 1/16 J.B.C. & A. Forms/C.2118/12.

WAR DIARY
or
INTELLIGENCE SUMMARY

Army Form C. 2118.

Volume 19
Page

Place	Date 1917	Hour	Summary of Events and Information	Remarks and references to Appendices
	Sept.	24.	Intr. Company relief.	
		25 to 28	Enemy artillery intermittently active, gas shells being used sometimes at night. Men out of trenches employed building Bat. Transport lines, Underway &c. Company relieved on night of 28/29 by 42 M.G. Coy. No casualties during the period.	
RAVELSBERG AREA		29	Company moved to Camp in RAVELSBERG AREA.	
		30	Cleaning up.	

Arthur Snowden Lieut
O.in C. 43 M.G. Coy.

Vol 20

WAR DIARY.

October 1917.

43rd Machine Gun Company.

Volume 20

WAR DIARY or INTELLIGENCE SUMMARY

Army Form C. 2118.

43 M.G. Coy.

Volume 20

Place	Date	Hour	Summary of Events and Information	Remarks and references to Appendices
RAVELSBERG AREA.	1917 Oct. 1		Cleaning up. Training when weather permitted.	
		2		
		3	Inspection by B.G.C. 43 Inf. Bde.	
		4	Packing up.	
N. of WESTOUTRE		5	Company moved to N. of WESTOUTRE	
		6	Bad weather prevented.	
		7	O.C.s inspection. Packing of Limbers.	
		8	Company moved to area N.W. of LA CLYTTE	
N.W. of LACLYTTE.		9	Preparing Guns for trenches.	
		10	Eight teams of 5 men each ten guns proceeded to BEDFORD HOUSE	
		11	preparatory to relieving 95th M.G. Coy. in sector front of PIEDERHOER CHATEAU	
		12	Relieved 95 M.G.Coy at 6 a.m. During the relief the 1st and 2nd Anzac Corps made an attack on our left under cover of a Smoke demonstration Barrage on our front. The enemy's retaliation caused 11 C.R. casualties amongst the teams which men were replaced by carrier.	
		13	During the day Coy. H.Q. heavily shelled. Intermittent enemy shelling all day also road. Enemy aircraft flying low over our trenches were engaged by our M.G.	

Army Form C. 2118.

WAR DIARY
or
INTELLIGENCE SUMMARY
(Erase heading not required.)

Page 2. Volume 20.

Place	Date 1917	Hour	Summary of Events and Information	Remarks and references to Appendices
N.W. POLDERHOEK CHATEAU.	Oct.	14.	Nothing beyond usual activity to report.	
		15.	Repeated heavy shelling of vicinity of Coy.H.A. 3 M Casualties caused here. Enemy counter-active but no infantry. M.G. targets were observed.	
		16.	Usual shelling & barrage fire. Enemy aeroplanes engaged by our M.G.	
	to			
		19.	Aeroplane bombs dropped near CAMERON COVERT nine. Enemy of 19 H.	
			M.G. located at Sq.H. of CHATEAU.	
		20.	Gas shells used during morning	
		21.	Nothing special to report.	
		22.	A bombardment of POLDERHOEK CHATEAU was arranged which necessitated a withdrawal from our front line to strenth ourselves from splinters. Two other M.Gs. (making a total of four) were placed in CAMERON COVERT with instructions to open fire on the evacuated area in order to prevent its occupation by the enemy. In addition the four Guns on the barrage positions in front of NORTHAMPTON FARM were laid on the same ground for the same purpose. Two Guns where normal positions were in front of the CHATEAU were also withdrawn, at the same time as the infantry to CARLISLE FARM being there operations a whole team Versene Counter. The Guns Teams	

Army Form C. 2118.

WAR DIARY
or
INTELLIGENCE SUMMARY Volume 20 Page 3

(Erase heading not required.)

Place	Date 1917	Hour	Summary of Events and Information	Remarks and references to Appendices
W. OF POPERINGHE CHATEAU (Cont.)	22		Returned to their original position at 5:30 P. During the day the Company suffered 10 casualties — 1 keep killed & 1 autogynous dying this wound.	
	23		Company were relieved by 15th M.G.Coy in the early morning. Relief was carried out without casualties. During this tour on the line generator were taken against Trench Feet &c — with the result that no cases of Trench Feet developed. On relief Company proceeded to trenches in SCOTTISH WOOD. Company moved to BERTHEN AREA in motor lorries.	
BERTHEN AREA	24 25 to 31		Training. 16 O.R. reinforcements arrived 30th.	

Ralph Nunn Lieut.
Cmdg 43 M.G. Coy

WAR DIARY.

43rd Machine Gun Company.

November 1917.

Volume 21.

Army Form C. 2118.

WAR DIARY
or
INTELLIGENCE SUMMARY

43rd M.G. Coy.

Volume 21

(Erase heading not required.)

Instructions regarding War Diaries and Intelligence Summaries are contained in F. S. Regs., Part II. and the Staff Manual respectively. Title Pages will be prepared in manuscript.

Page 1

Place	Date	Hour	Summary of Events and Information	Remarks and references to Appendices
BERTHEN AREA.	Nov. 1. 1917	} 5 12 13	Training. One Parade scheme for Officers was carried out during the period. An average of 15 to 20 men were in hospital withdrawn in this area. Company moved by Rail to Second Army Training area, being billeted at WESTBÉCOURT.	
WESTBÉCOURT.	14	} 6 30	Training. Special attention paid to Physical training, Barrage drill, M.G. in open &c, &c. Three Officers evacuated sick during this period. Three Officers reinforcements.	

Ralph Moore Capt.
O.md. 43 M.G. Coy.

WAR DIARY.
****

43rd Machine Gun Company.
****

December 1917.
****

Volume 22.
****

Army Form C. 2118.

WAR DIARY
or
INTELLIGENCE SUMMARY

113th M.G. Company
Volume 22

Page 1

(Erase heading not required.)

Place	Date	Hour	Summary of Events and Information	Remarks and references to Appendices
WESTBECOURT.	Dec 1		Training. Packing Limbers &C. Transport moved off last inst.	
	2		to VLAMERTINGHE Area.	
		3.	Company moved by train to ST. JEAN.	
ST. JEAN.		4		
		5	In reserve. Guns prepared for trench mts.	
		8		
		9.	Company relieved 41 M.G. Coy in the line. 9 positions. Two turnage positions were also relieved, personnel being attached to 224 M.G. Coy. Relief was complete by 7am. 1 O.R. casualty (killed). The day was comparatively quiet with intervals of shelling chiefly in neighbourhood of MEETCHEELE and BELLEVUE.	
NE PASSCHENDAELE		10	Heavy hostile shelling over whole area must heavy was mostly	
		11.	Enemy shelling very heavy at intervals. An endeavour to assist in location of our forces by enemy was made while some new gun positions for aeroplane photography. No contact was	

2449 Wt. W14957/Mgo 750,000 1/16 J.B.C. & A. Forms/C.2118/12.

Army Form C. 2118.

WAR DIARY
or
INTELLIGENCE SUMMARY
(Erase heading not required.)

Page 2.

Place	Date	Hour	Summary of Events and Information	Remarks and references to Appendices
NE PASSCHENDAELE	Dec. 11 1917		Unfavourable turn of activities by E.A. An enemy barrage was placed immediately in HEETCHELE. At 11am lasted 15 minutes. Being preceded by a bombardment of Enj. MG pill box. Twelve heavy shells per minute were counted. Ruin enemy was held up by Gas shells.	
	12		Quieter day. Rain. Enemy was held up by Gas shells. 2 t.R. wounded in barrage position.	
	13		H. SKENT killed at MOSSELMARKT. Enemy MGs active. L. ANDERSON and two team relieved owing to exposed position. Team relieved owing to 6 H.G. on	
	14		Normal. Night firing was carried out by 6 M.G. on selected targets during enemy divisional relief	
	15		Quieter day	
	16		Company relieved by 41 M.G.Coy. Relief completed by 8am. Company moved back in reserve to BRANDHOEK.	
	"		Fort Stopholton have been carried out during the whole	
BRANDHOEK	17 to 20		In reserve. No operations have been carried out of period since 14/12/17	
	21		Company moved to Camp South of WIELTJE. 41st Company relieved on the line with two teams on barrage positions	

2449 Wt. W14957/M90 750,000 1/16 J.B.C. & A. Forms/C.2118/12.

WAR DIARY
or
INTELLIGENCE SUMMARY.

Army Form C. 2118.

Page 3

Place	Date	Hour	Summary of Events and Information	Remarks and references to Appendices
N.E. PASSCHENDAELE	22		Day fairly quiet. 1 O.R. killed by shell fire.	
	23		Some hostile fire & heavy snowfall.	
	24		Quiet during the day but harassing fire on tracks & areas during the night.	
	25		1 O.R. wounded & 1 O.R. missing. These casualties happened to return party which lost its way.	
	26		Considerable gas shelling. H.Q. shelled for 3 hours with 8" shells. Infantry relief during night caused enemy to open barrage with M.G.s & artillery.	
	27		Company relieved by 23 M.G. Coy. 1 Lt E.K. Mitchell wounded during relief.	
NESTBÉ COURT	28		Company moved by lorry to NESTBÉ COURT. Heavy snows caused considerable difficulty with transport.	
	29 to 31		Xmas dinners held on 31st.	

W.T. Innes Lieut
and/43 M.G. Coy.

No 23

War Diary

of

43" Machine Gun Coy

to

January 1918.

Volume 32

Army Form C. 2118.

WAR DIARY
or
INTELLIGENCE SUMMARY.
(Erase heading not required.)

43 M.G. Coy
Vol. 23
Page 1

Instructions regarding War Diaries and Intelligence Summaries are contained in F. S. Regs., Part II. and the Staff Manual respectively. Title pages will be prepared in manuscript.

Place	Date 1918	Hour	Summary of Events and Information	Remarks and references to Appendices
WESTBÉCOURT	Jan. 1.		Company marched to TATINGHEM.	
TATINGHEM	2.		Company marched to ST OMER entrained with transport detachment	
		7-30pm	at EDGEHILLE (SOMME) & marched to BRAY S/SOMME.	
BRAY S/SOMME	3		Resting - cleaning up	
	4 to 21st		Training in G.H.Q. reserve.	
	22nd		Company & Transport marched to GUIVUCOURT.	
GUIVUCOURT	23		" " " GUISCARD	
GUISCARD	24		" " " FLAVY-LE-MARTEL	
FLAVY-LE-MARTEL	25		" " " REMIGNY	
REMIGNY	26		10 Guns with teams & 80 men relieved 10 Guns & French in sector N. & S. of MOŸ during evening. Relief was carried out without incident. Transport & Coy HQ (Temporary) billeted at REMIGNY.	
	27 to 31		Very quiet. Nothing to report except fair amount of E.A. activity. Slight enemy artillery activity might both with with few gas shells.	

W. Imes Lieut
Cmdg 43 M.G. Coy.

Vol 24

War Diary.

43rd Machine Gun Coy.

February 1918

Volume 24

Army Form C. 2118.

WAR DIARY
or
INTELLIGENCE SUMMARY.   43 M.G.Coy.
(Erase heading not required.)   Vol. 24

Page 1.

Place	Date	Hour	Summary of Events and Information	Remarks and references to Appendices
MOY Secteur	1918 Feby.1.	1.	Quiet. Some enemy M.G. fire during around J ration.	
		2.	Registry carried out by enemy artillery. Quiet. Internal company relief 6 p.m.	
		3.	Considerable E.A. activity. E.A. flew low over MOY fired at troops.	
		4.	Worthy of report. Increase in enemy artillery fire during day & evening.	
		5.	Normal.	
		6.	Nothing to report.	
		7.	Internal company relief 6 p.m. Slight artillery activity during day.	
		8.		
		9.	Normal.	
		10.		
		11.	Considerable E.A. activity — mostly out of range of M.G.	
		12 to 14.	Very Quiet. Internal company relief 6 p.m.–10 p.m.	
		15.	E.A. activity. One driven off by A.A. M.G.	

Army Form C. 2118.

WAR DIARY
or
INTELLIGENCE SUMMARY.
(Erase heading not required.)

Page 2.

Place	Date 1918	Hour	Summary of Events and Information	Remarks and references to Appendices
Mot Ecto.	Feb.	16	Some shelling. E.A. activity.	
		17	M.G. active against E.A. Some shelling.	
		18	Enemy trench mortared trenches. N.T.M.'s at 4 a.m. 1 O.R. wounded.	
		19	Slight aerial activity. Inter-company relief night 20/21.	
		20	Normal. Slight enemy shelling.	
		21		
		22	Some aerial activity. Enemy M.G. active by one of ours.	
		23	Quiet.	
		24		
		25	Company relieved by 53 M.G. Coy. Proceeded to JUSSY.	
JUSSY		26	Resting & training. Coy. in Bn. Reserve.	
		to		
		28		

W. Innes Lieut.
O in Cmdg 3 M.G. Coy.

www.ingramcontent.com/pod-product-compliance
Lightning Source LLC
Chambersburg PA
CBHW081434160426
43193CB00013B/2280